Ben's tooth

Story by Beverley Randell
Illustrated by Genevieve Rees

Ben was eating an apple
at school.

"Ow!" he said. "Oh, look!
My tooth has (come) out . . .
and here it is, in my apple!"

Ben went to show his teacher.
"Look, Mrs. Green," he said.
"My tooth has come out."

"Here's a little box
to put it in," said Mrs. Green.

Ben ran home after school
and showed Mom.

"Look at me," he said.

"Where is your tooth?"
said Mom.
"Have you got it?"

Anthropology

THE AQUATIC APE

Paintings of Early Man

8

"It's here," said Ben,
"in this little box."

"Good," said Mom.
"The tooth fairy
   may come and get it
   after you go to sleep.
   Put it by your bed."

9

"A fairy?" said Ben. "A fairy?
Fairies are in fairy tales.
They can't come into my bedroom
and get my tooth.
You are **silly**, Mom."

Mom laughed.

At bedtime
Ben put his tooth by his bed.
"A fairy won't come," he said.
Mom read him a story
and he went to sleep.

Will a fairy come?
Will she? Or won't she?

In the morning Ben woke up.
He looked in the little box . . .

"My tooth has gone," he said,
"and there is some **money**
in my little box!"

"Mom! Come and see!"
he called.